Yorgos Maraziotis

NIGHT OF THE WORLD

MER. Paper Kunsthalle

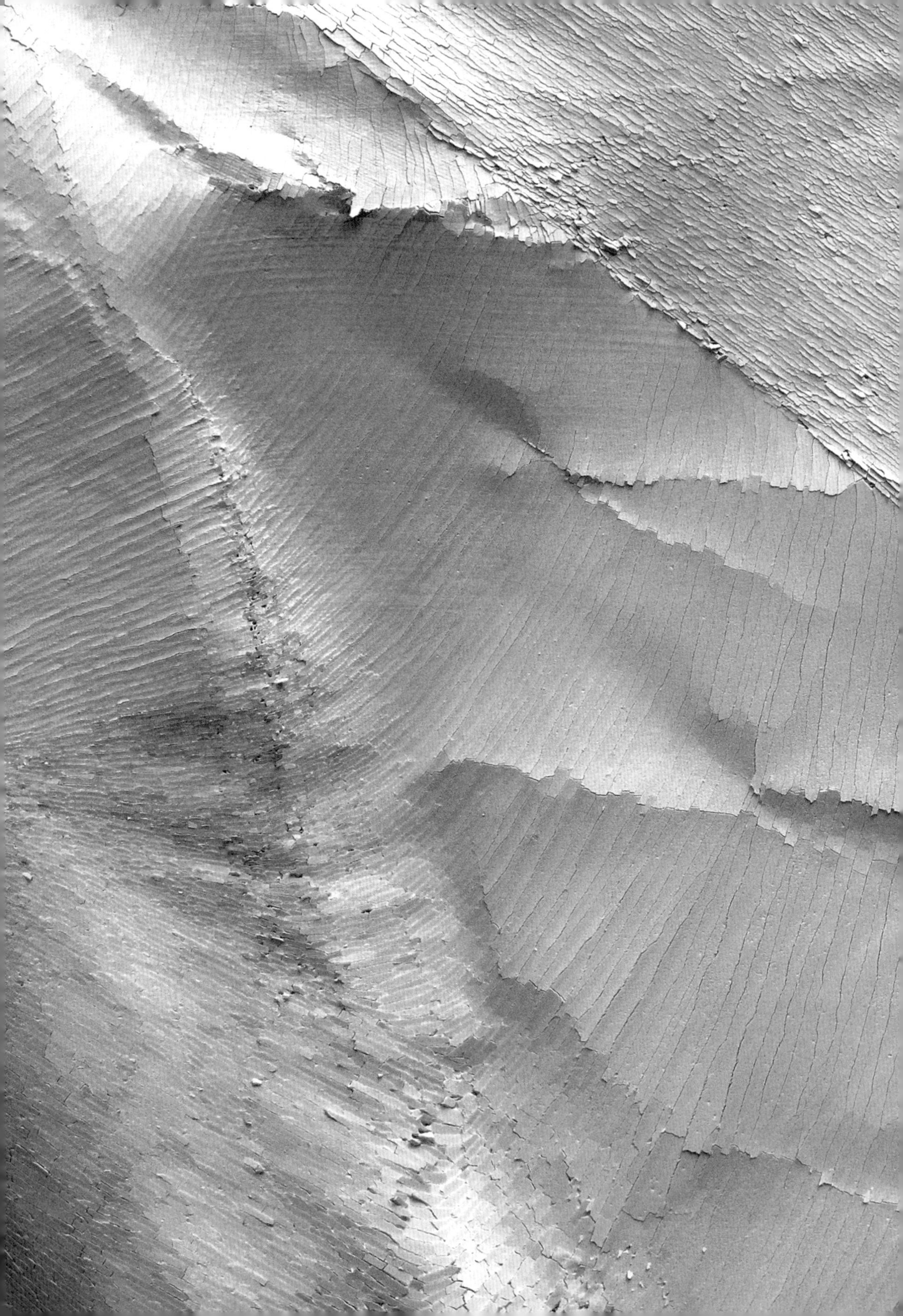

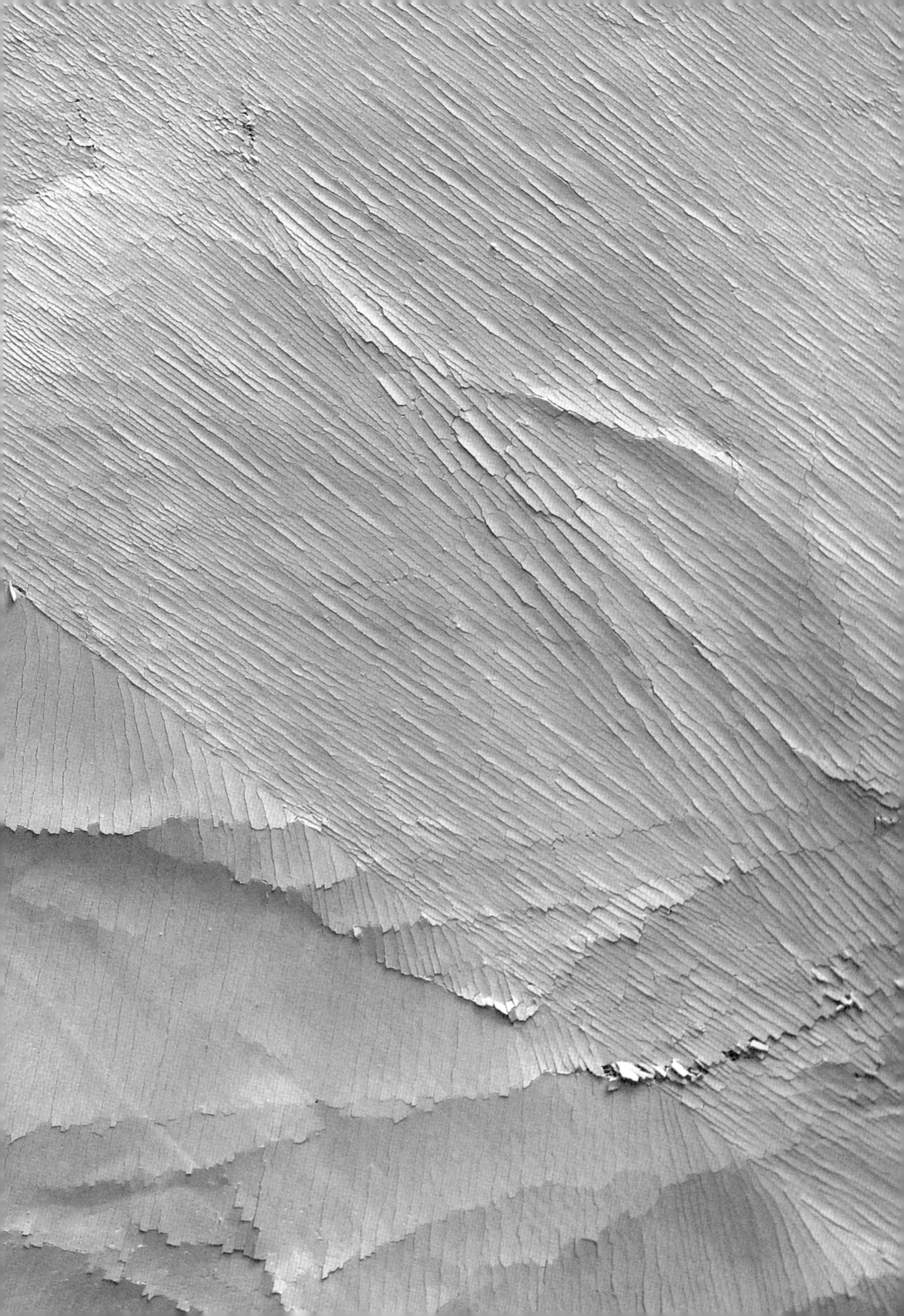

The human being is this night, this empty nothing, that contains everything in its simplicity - an unending wealth of many presentations, images, of which none happens to occur to him - or which are not present. This night, the inner of nature, that exists here - pure self - in phantasmagorical presentations, is night all around it, here shoots a bloody head - there another white shape, suddenly here before it, and just so disappears. One catches sight of this night when one looks human beings in the eye - into a night that becomes awful, it suspends the night of the world here in an opposition. In this night, being has returned.

From the manuscript of Georg Wilhelm Friedrich Hegel, Realphilosophie 1805–1806

Ο άνθρωπος είναι αυτή η νύχτα, αυτό το άδειο τίποτα, που περικλείει τα πάντα στην απλότητά του – ένας πλούτος απείρως πολλών παραστάσεων, εικόνων από τις οποίες καμία δεν τυχαίνει να του συμβαίνει – ή που δεν είναι πια παρούσες. Αυτή η νύχτα, το εσώτερον της φύσης που υπάρχει ενθαδικά – το καθαρό ταυτό– σε φαντασμαγορικές παραστάσεις, είναι η νύχτα που είναι τριγύρω του, εδώ μια αιματηρή κεφαλή ξεπροβάλει ξαφνικά – εκεί μια άλλη λευκή μορφή, και έτσι επίσης εξαφανίζεται. Μπορεί να αντικρίσει κανείς αυτή τη νύχτα όταν κοιτά τον άνθρωπο κατάματα – μέσα σε μια νύχτα που γίνεται τρομερή – άρει τη νύχτα του κόσμου ενθαδικά σε μια αντίφαση. Σε αυτή τη νύχτα το ον, έχει επιστρέψει.

Από το χειρόγραφο του Georg Wilhelm Friedrich Hegel, Φυσική Φιλοσοφία και Φιλοσοφία του Πνεύματος 1805-1806

ON HYPERMODERN PHOBIAS AND SUPER-HUMAN ACTS

Sotirios Bahtsetzis

"The broader one's understanding, the greater the plethora of different kinds of beauty one is receptive to." Blaise Pascal

The rejection of art - consider phrases such as "I don't understand it" or "I don't need it", phrases you may probably have already heard from a viewer of a contemporary art work - is very much a symptom of that greatest of fears prevailing in our lives: the fear of death. A rejection of today's art indicates an effort to renounce the mortality of our existence. A statement such as this may sound rather provocative and therefore needs further explanation.

According to philosopher Kostas Axelos, if art was once marked by nature, god and Man (creating in each era either an ancient Greek sculpture, a romanesque church or the portrait of a Renaissance man) (34), then what could someone do after the proclaimed end of art -according to Hegel- in order to substantiate its attachment to the world? Let us consider that every certainty about the world is a symptom of our supreme imaginary attachment to an absurd belief that we will continue to exist even after the world ceases to for us. All monotheistic religions, all political utopias and, ultimately, every type of ontology capitalize on precisely this culturally widespread belief, the keystone of Western civilization: the belief in the infinite continuation of both "Man" as a species, as well as of every single one of us by means of whichever kind of posthumous fame we may be able to secure for ourselves.

But when Nietzsche pronounced the death of God, by which he was essentially referring to the end of mankind, he brought us before an important question: How would Nietzsche's new man, the super-human of hypermodernity (the two concepts are basically one and the same) be able to "do" anything? And Axelos goes on to add: "In the era of the will for power and the will for willpower, the will wants to conquer the Whole. But what happens with the Zero? It is the will that wants us to do art, as we are willing to do that or the other, as long as we do something". (42) In an attempt to give an answer to this, we could say that in our times, only the will - and therefore art - that opens itself up to the Zero, to non-certainty, to the absence of foundation and to what the young Hegel once called "the night of the world", may be able to "do".

The rejection of art for the Nietzschean man is the symptom of regression to a fantasy that both we and our civilization will be able to conquer the Whole -by making sculptures, churches, portraits- perpetuating ad infinitum the belief in the continuity of this world and the supposed transcendence of death (yes, it is indeed difficult for someone to be living in the age of the end of Man!). Axelos, however, urges us rather than reject death "to come to terms with it, to live it and to take it on with affection" (44). The non- rejection of death constitutes in reality the acceptance of art (i.e. the will) produced by this novel man. Only he, this post-human who does not hope for a posthumous "restoration of everything", nor vegetates in the artificial and nihilistic oblivion of a contemporary "pragmatism" whose bliss lasts as long as one TV commercial, may be the one capable of "doing", after all values and frames of reference have been lost.

And behold...! The ideal viewer of Yorgos Maraziotis' newest work stands before you. In the artist's recent work, the iconological references to some kind of theology, for example the three handmade nails on a white wall (one of the seven items- symbols of Arma Christi, emblematic representations of the passion of Christ), or the heap of a particularly flammable black powder (ground coal) on a white pedestal (a reference to a global symbol of memento mori), or even a wall piece of white marble (perhaps as a memorial or funerary inscription) no doubt constitute the simplest way of an interpretive approach to his thought. Indeed, the artist comments on loss, death, or the negative aspect of the human condition transmit to the viewer a feeling of sanctity and awe as befits such a subject. But this visual commentary does not constitute a denial or a rejection of this negativity so much as an acceptance of the limits to our existence.

Various emblematic symbols - a broken light bulb in the corner of the exhibition space (perhaps the equivalent of a snuffed candle as seen in a Baroque painting), a white modern "fossil" (made out of gesso) on the ground – all refer to the feeling of human permeability, transience and fragility summarized in that striking quote by the first avant la lettre existentialist philosopher, Blaise Pascal, that "man is nothing but a reed, the weakest thing in nature", a quotation which nevertheless captures its very tragicness with the explanation "...but a thinking reed!".

And indeed: in an almost vacant room, we encounter the neon sign NOW, a reference to the concept of present time, which exists only as a conceptual abstraction: the 'now' is what happens between the 'shortly before' and the 'shortly after', but never exists on its own or autonomously. Perhaps the most commonplace word of everyday use reveals itself to be as hollow as Pascal's reed. Our only resistance to the permeability of linear time, the absurdity of existence itself, is the duration of our contemplation in front of a mirror in the centre of the room: not our reflection on the surface of the mirror, but the length of our inspection in it.

All the works of the artist operate precisely within these boundaries of inspection while at the same time taking into account the semiotics of its media. In his black & white silkscreen prints, simple forms take on a 3D character: designs become textures inviting the viewer to touch them. Standing in front of other prints, the viewer is required to shift from the usual frontal view standing position - a small step to the left or right - in order for "a cry of a face captured within the white" to be revealed. A 'now' trapped in the time dimension of our sensory inspection. The materials themselves also take part in this game of boundaries: the sharp cruelty of an ice- berg or fence wire, a "white cry", a marble plate or a shattered piece of glass, they all lose their threatening status. The sensorial metamorphosis of the Dionysian to the Apollonian, of ecstasy and chaos into an evocative harmony and grace, very much a speculative kind of post- modern acceptance of the romantic ideal, opens up new spaces for meditation.

If someone should speak today of romanticism, they might mention the element of emotional visionarism, an inherent characteristic of this pre-modern era of thought. The re-invention of this affect is an imperative necessity, just because art from 1960 onwards has ostracised affect, either for fear of being accused as contributing to the entertainment industry (and therefore labelled 'kitsch'), or out of excessive belief in its conceptual, that is, Hegelian, destiny (and therefore labelled 'formalism'). And this type of affect today can be nothing but post-modern: an icy, white cry, an archaic smile on the surface of the mirror, a hint of absence in gesso. It is with such kinds of affect that the artist invites us to negotiate or respond to the imperatives of today, which are close to what the young Hegel called the "night of the world" i.e. the absurd negativity, the horrifying contingency of the actual. And even if later on the same philosopher prefixed an enormous reasoning, as stated by Slavoj Žižek (15), the ghost of which for two centuries now both philosophy and art have been struggling to oppose, this initial statement has never ceased to be of great importance, constituting as it does a primary point of identification for the deeply contradictory character of reality and the decentered essence of man. Perhaps in line with Hegel - or not - we could nowadays say that even if the 'I' is always outside its self, deeply heteronomous, existing fundamentally in relation to the Other, this relationship to the Other, which is of decisive importance in the human condition, might ultimately not be one of struggle but of love. This may be where the deeper significance of a white cry lies, when this cry opposes itself to the night of the world in an effort to transcend it, not by abolishing its darkness, but the way in which we receive the absence of light. And let us not forget: Cosmology has proven that the night sky is in fact one of glaring brightness and full of stars, only our eyes are unable to see this cosmic light.

Bibliography: Kostas Axelos, *The Opening to the upcoming and the Opening of art*, Nefeli editions, Athens 2009 and Slavoj Žižek, *Psychoanalyse und die Philosophie des deutschen Idealismus (I. Der erhabenste aller Hysteriker, II. Verweilen beim Negativen)*, Vienna, Turia & Kant, 2008.

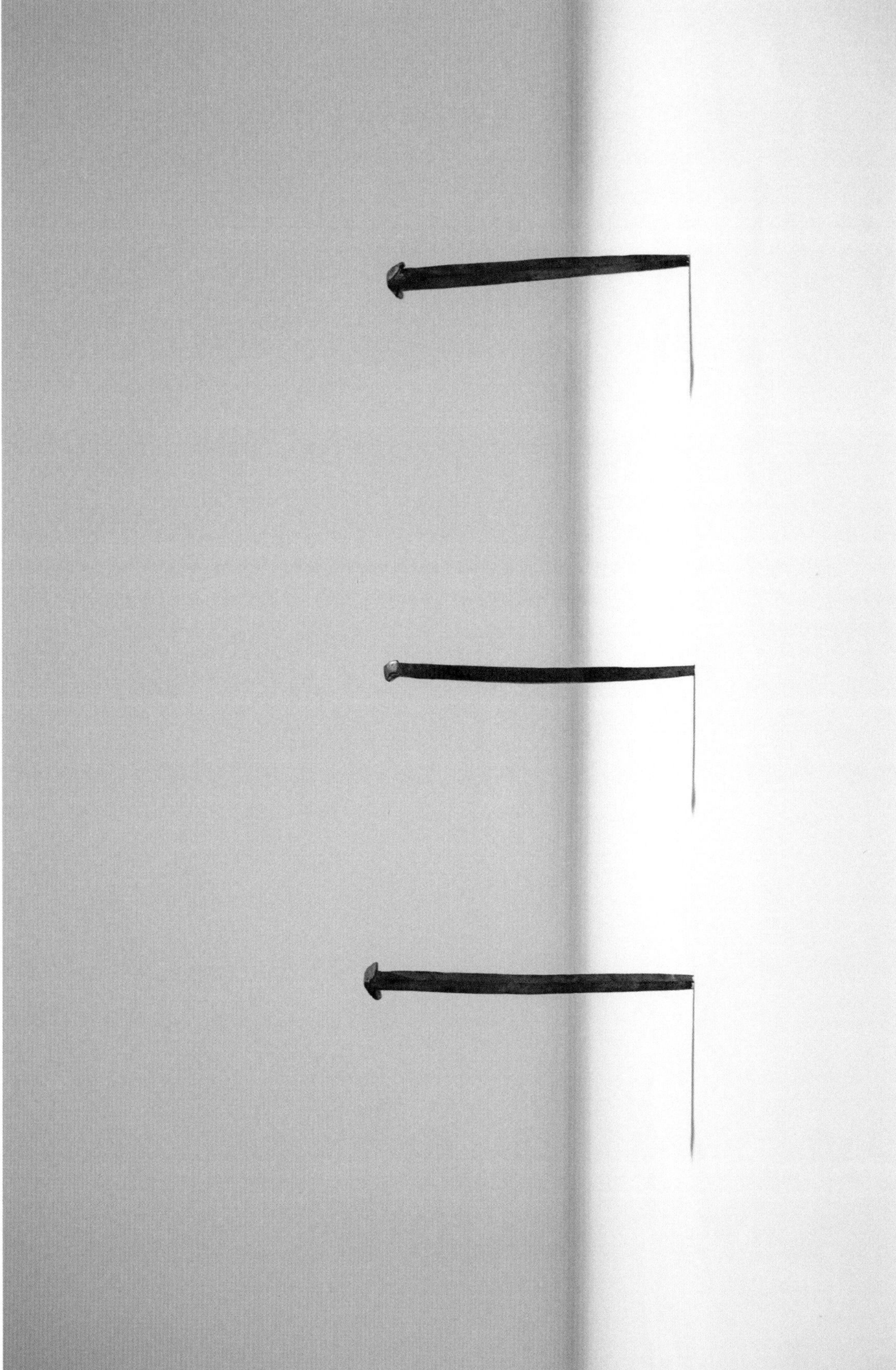

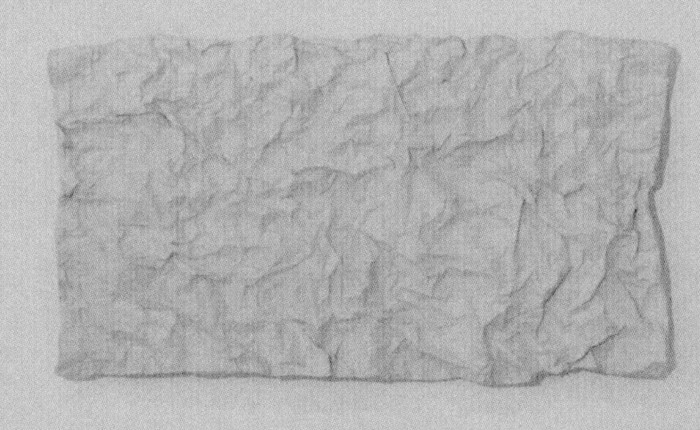

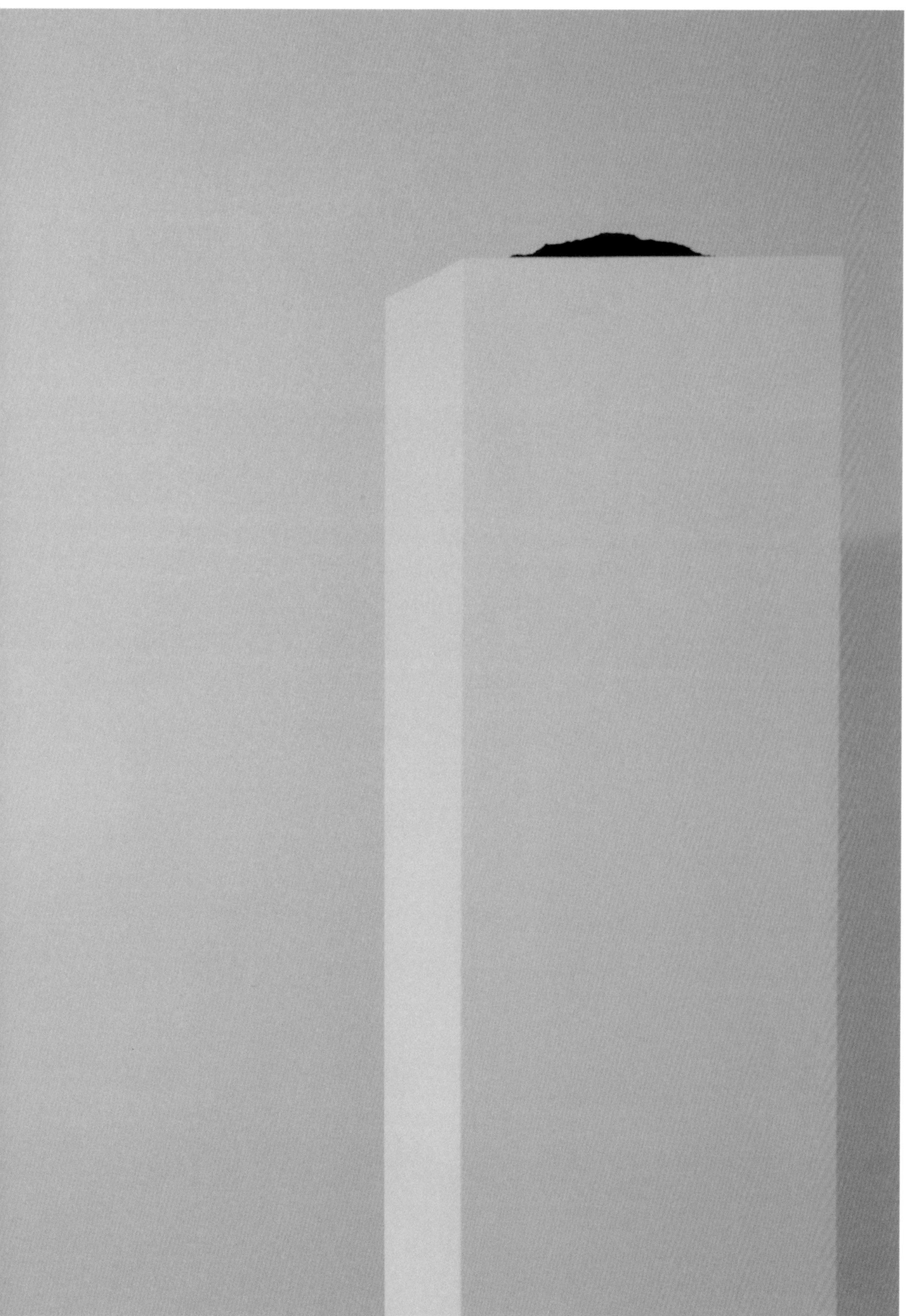

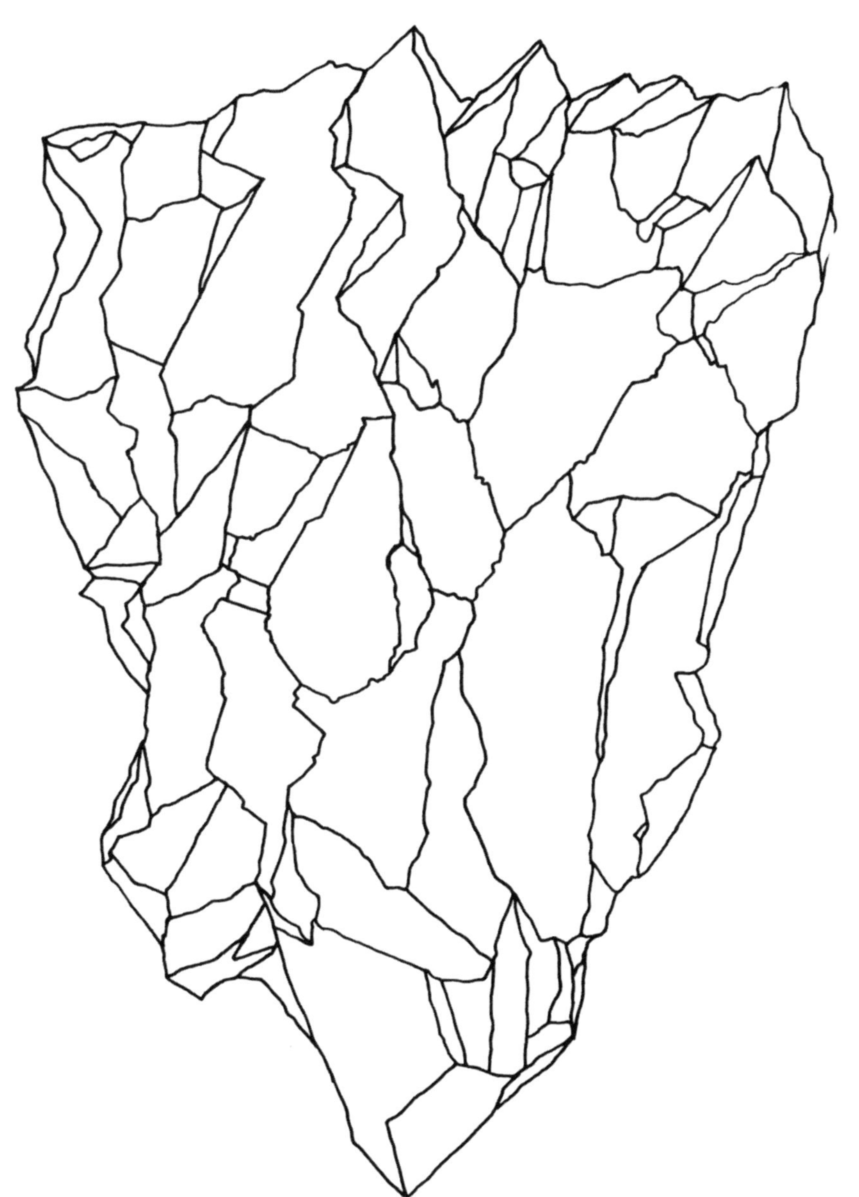

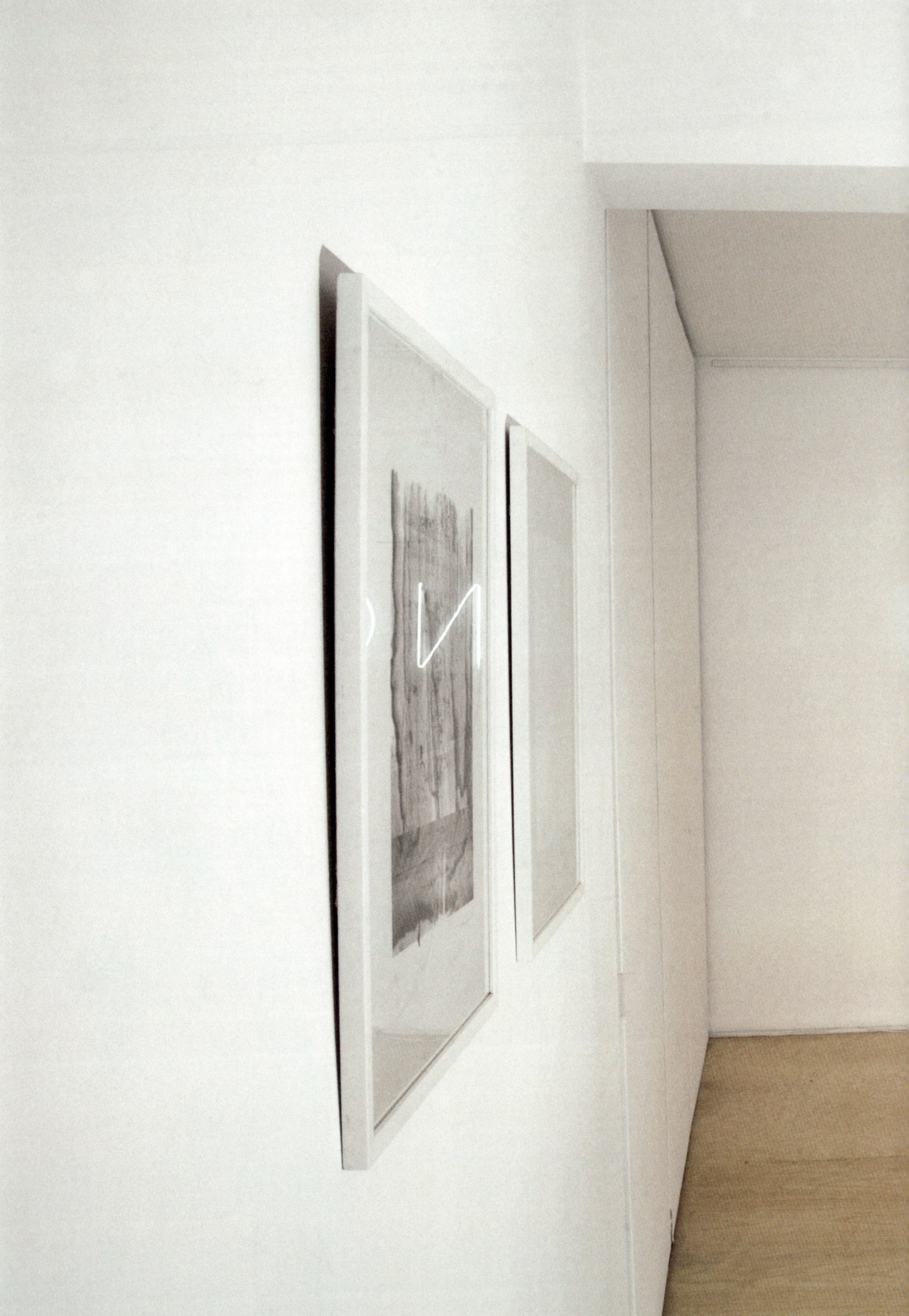

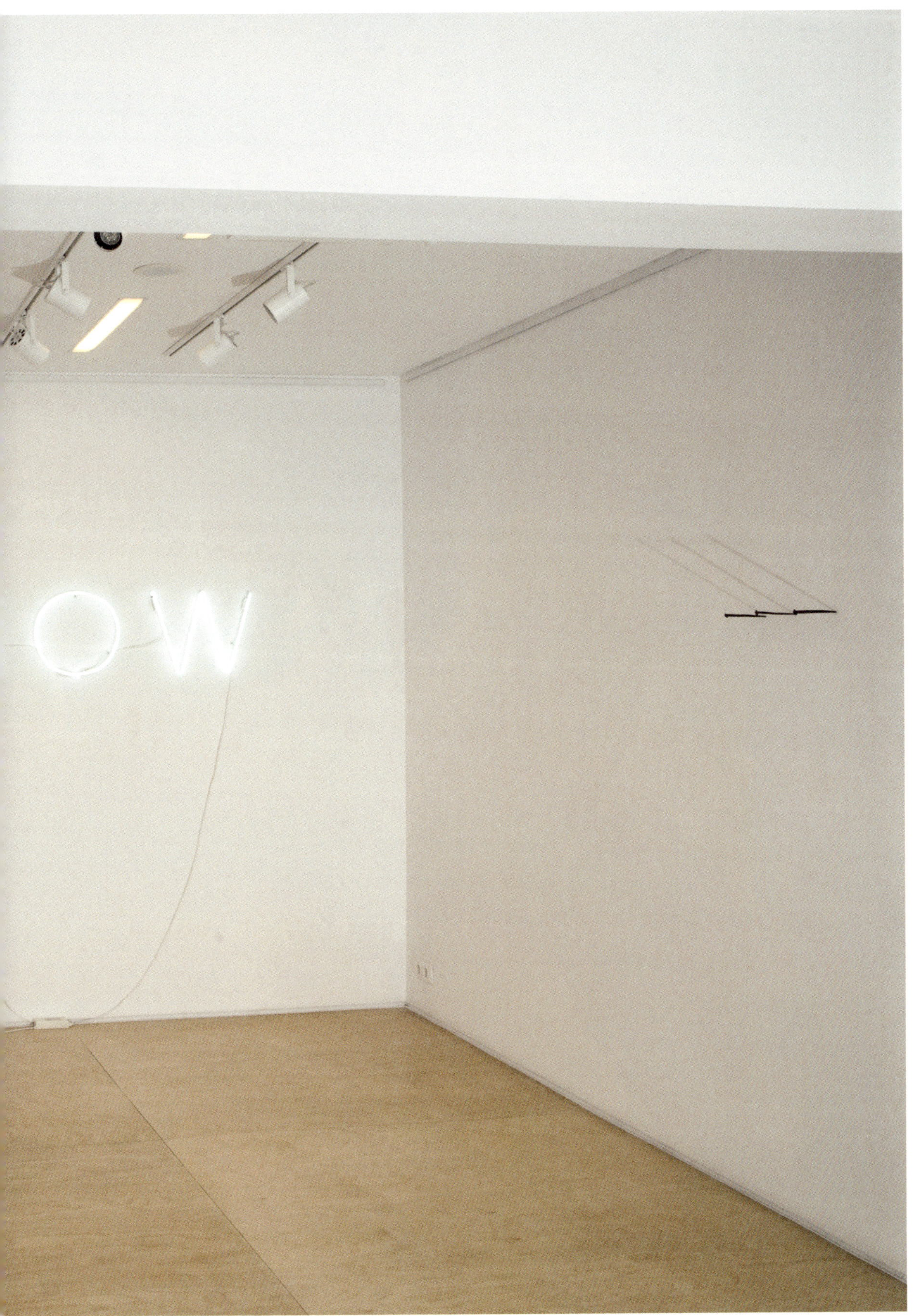

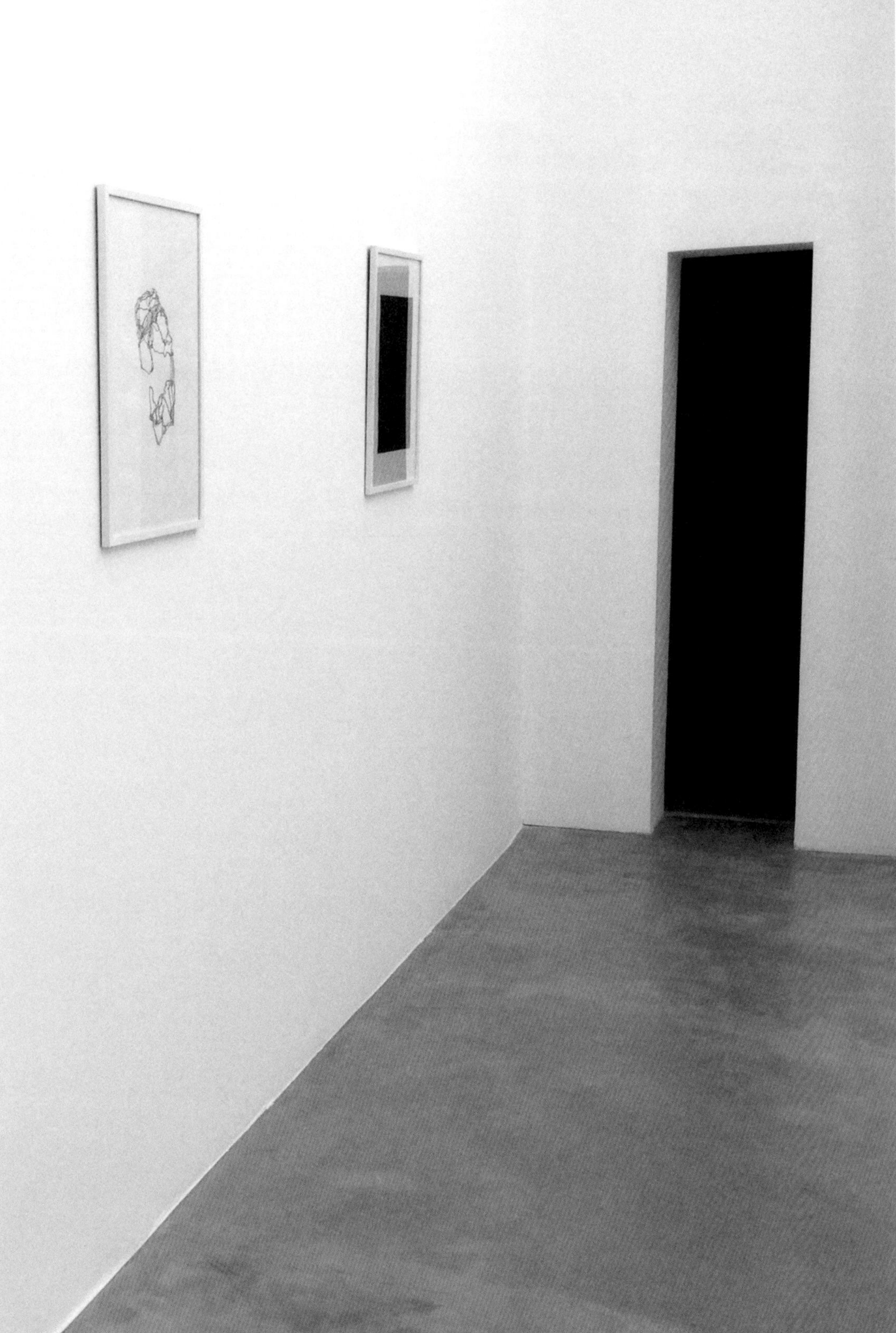

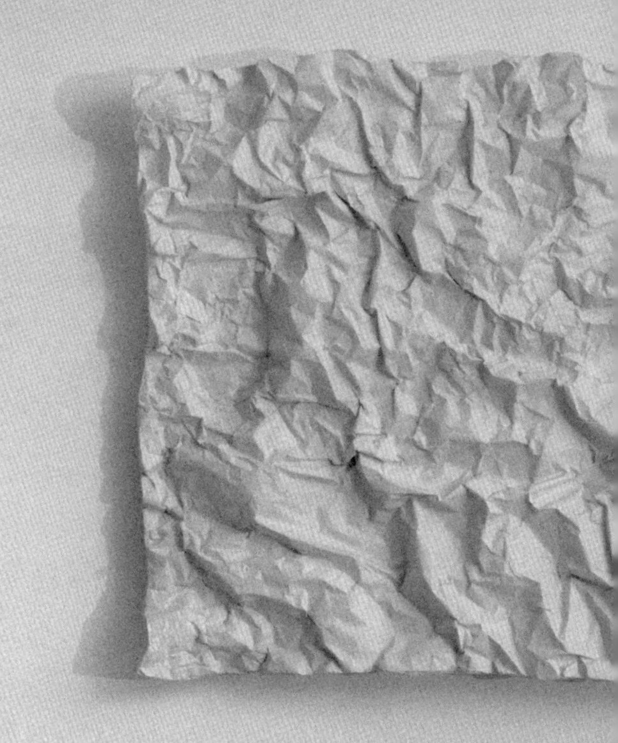

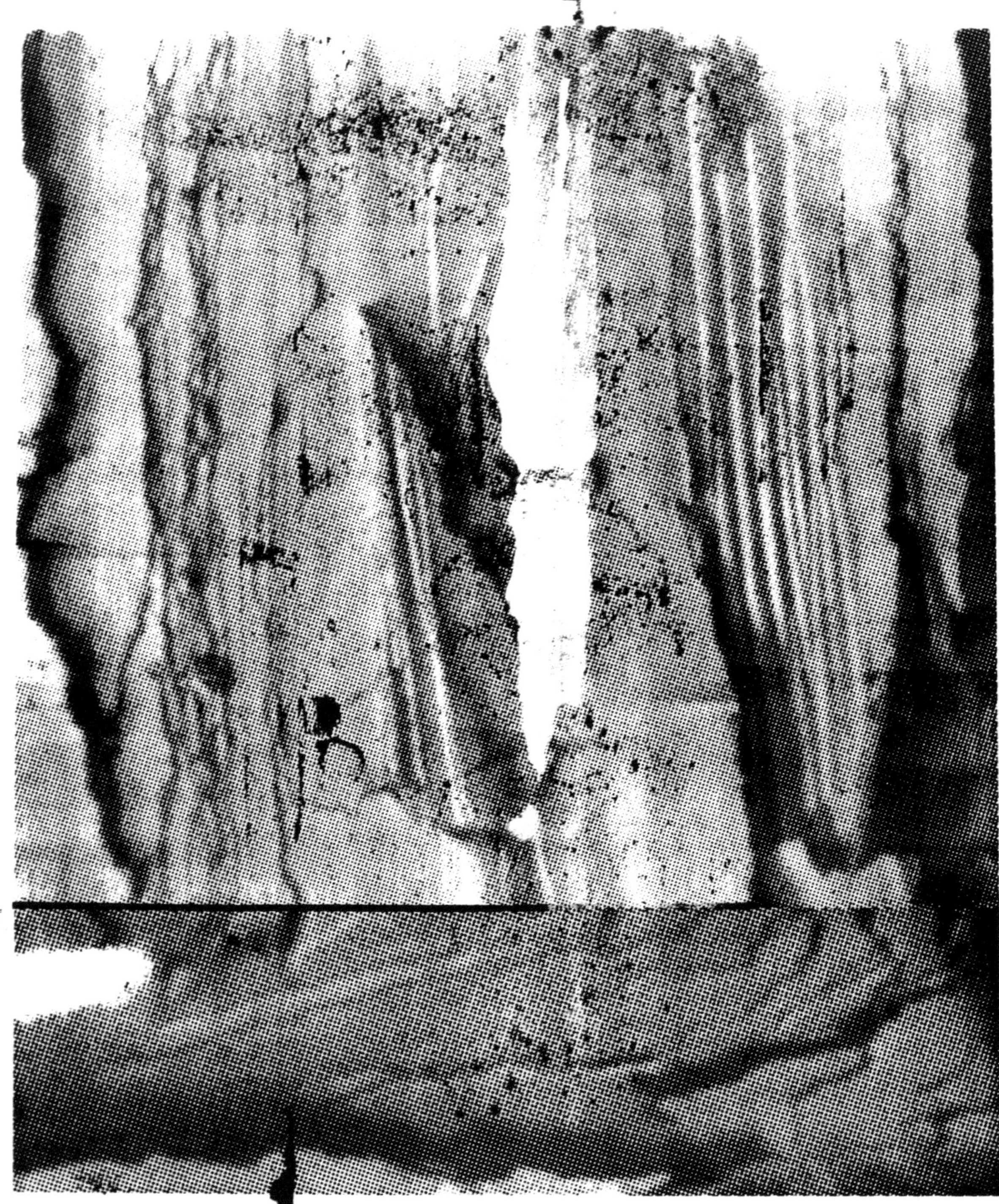

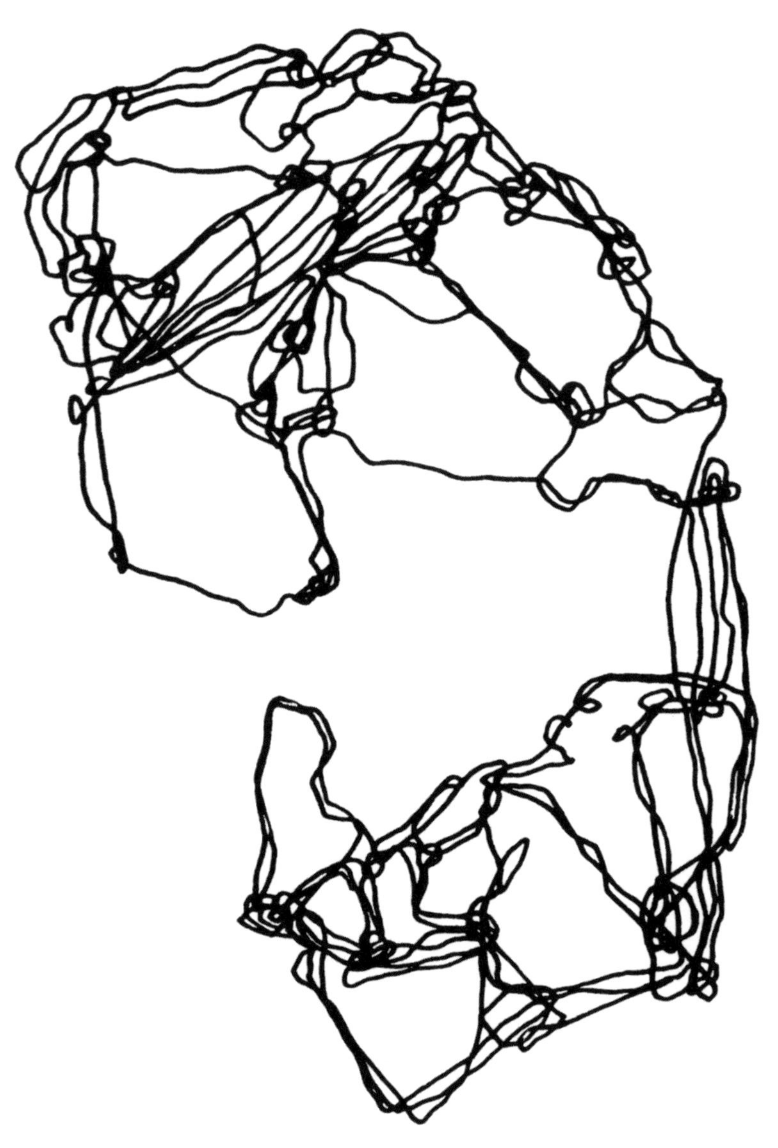

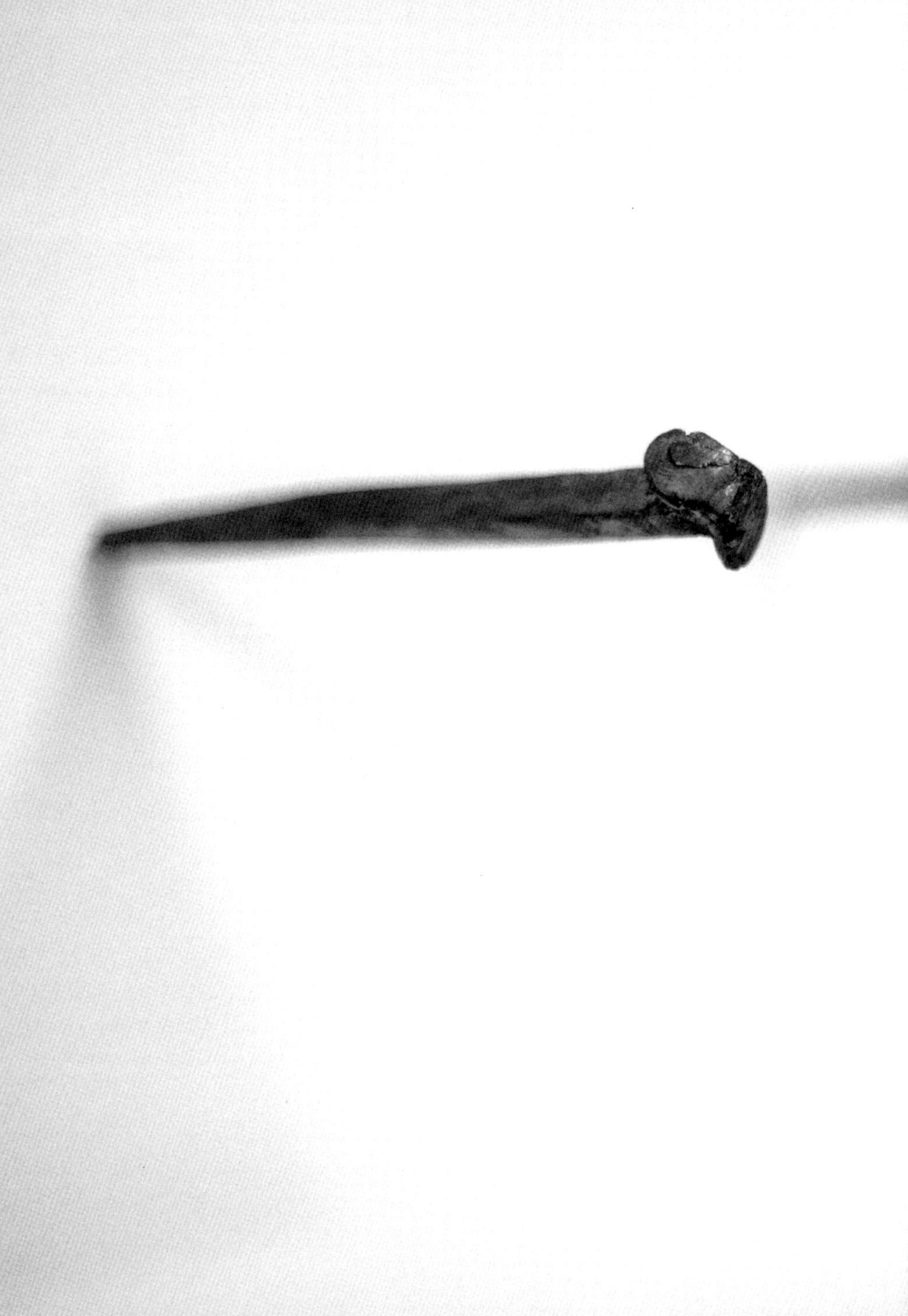

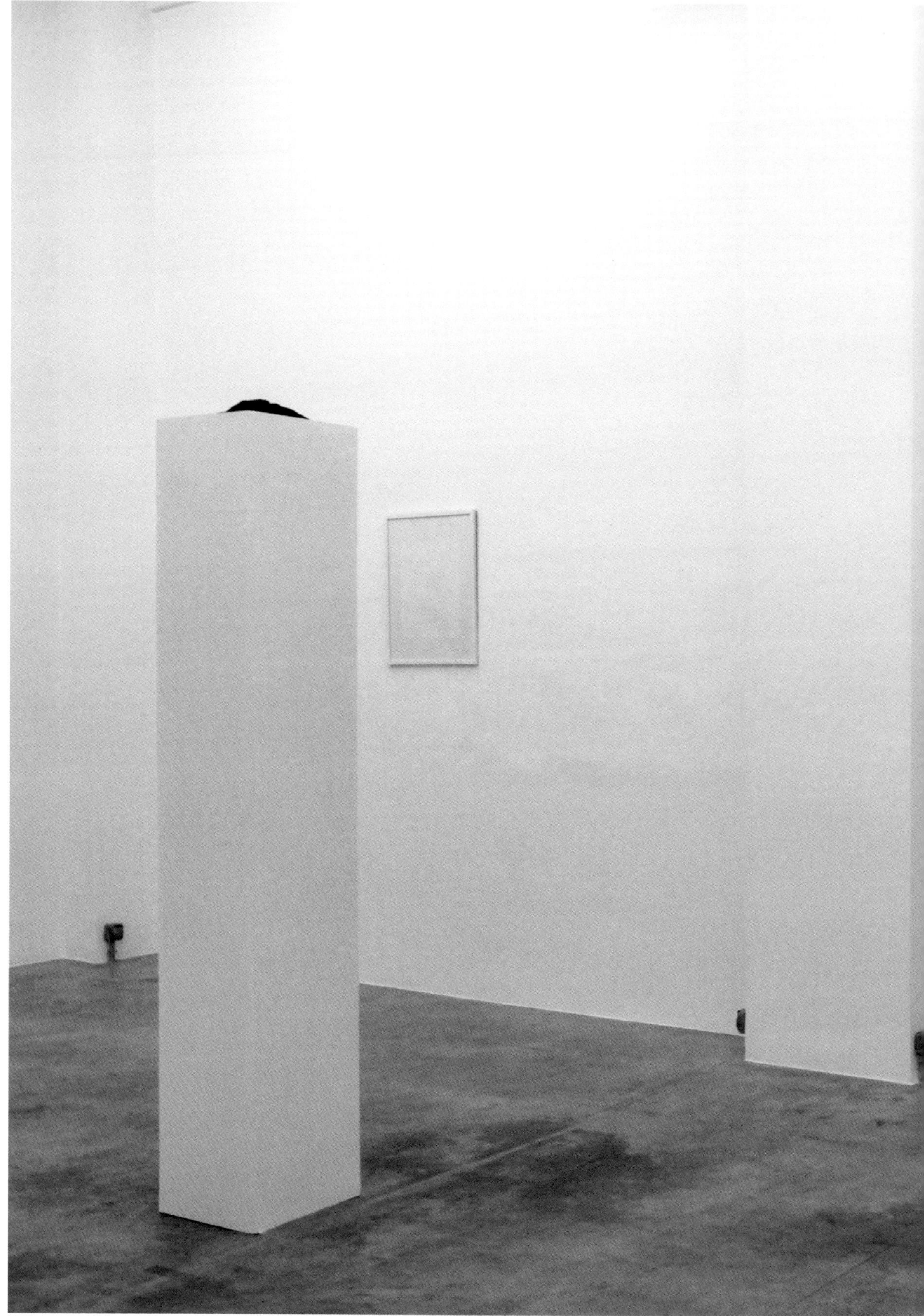

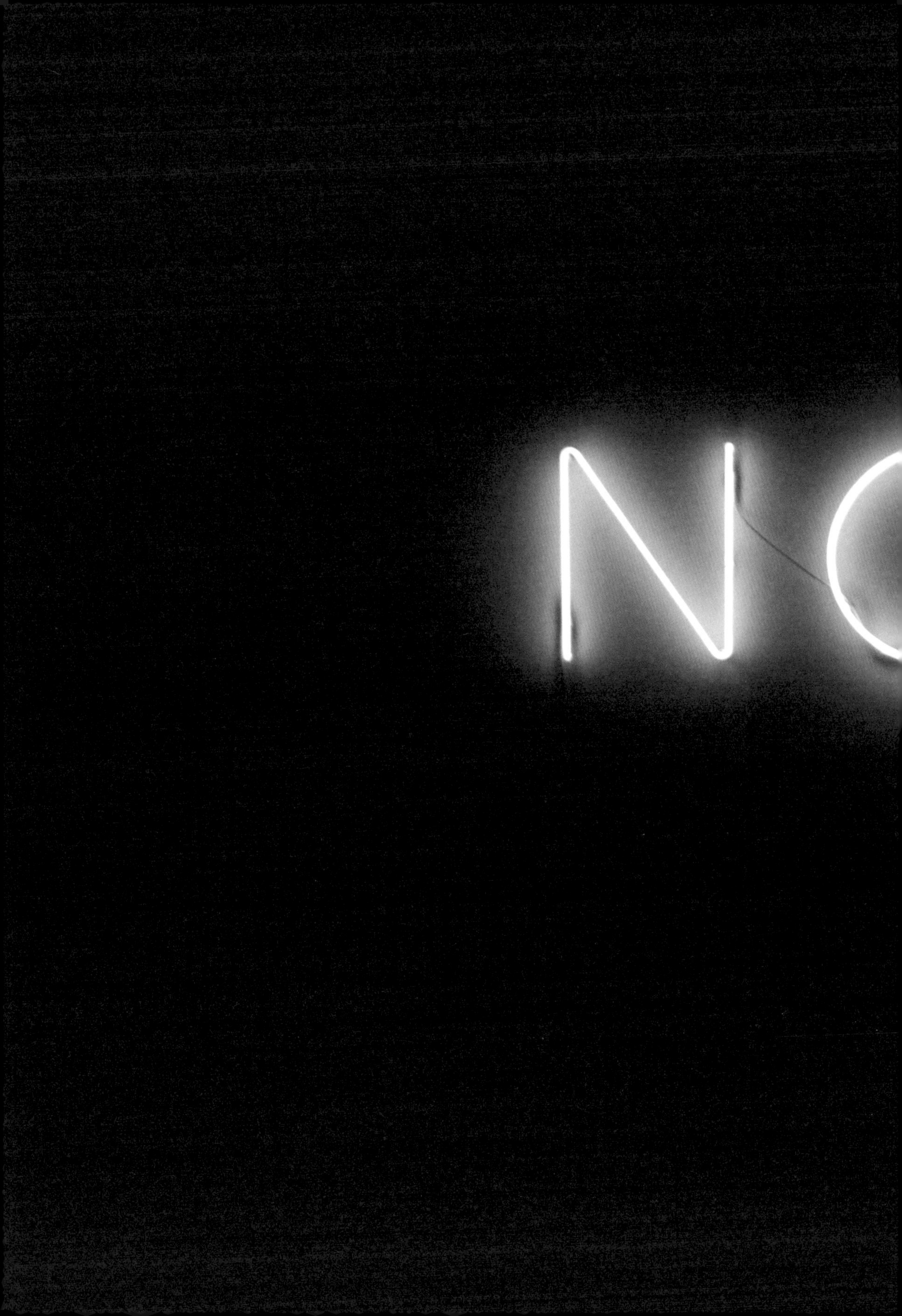

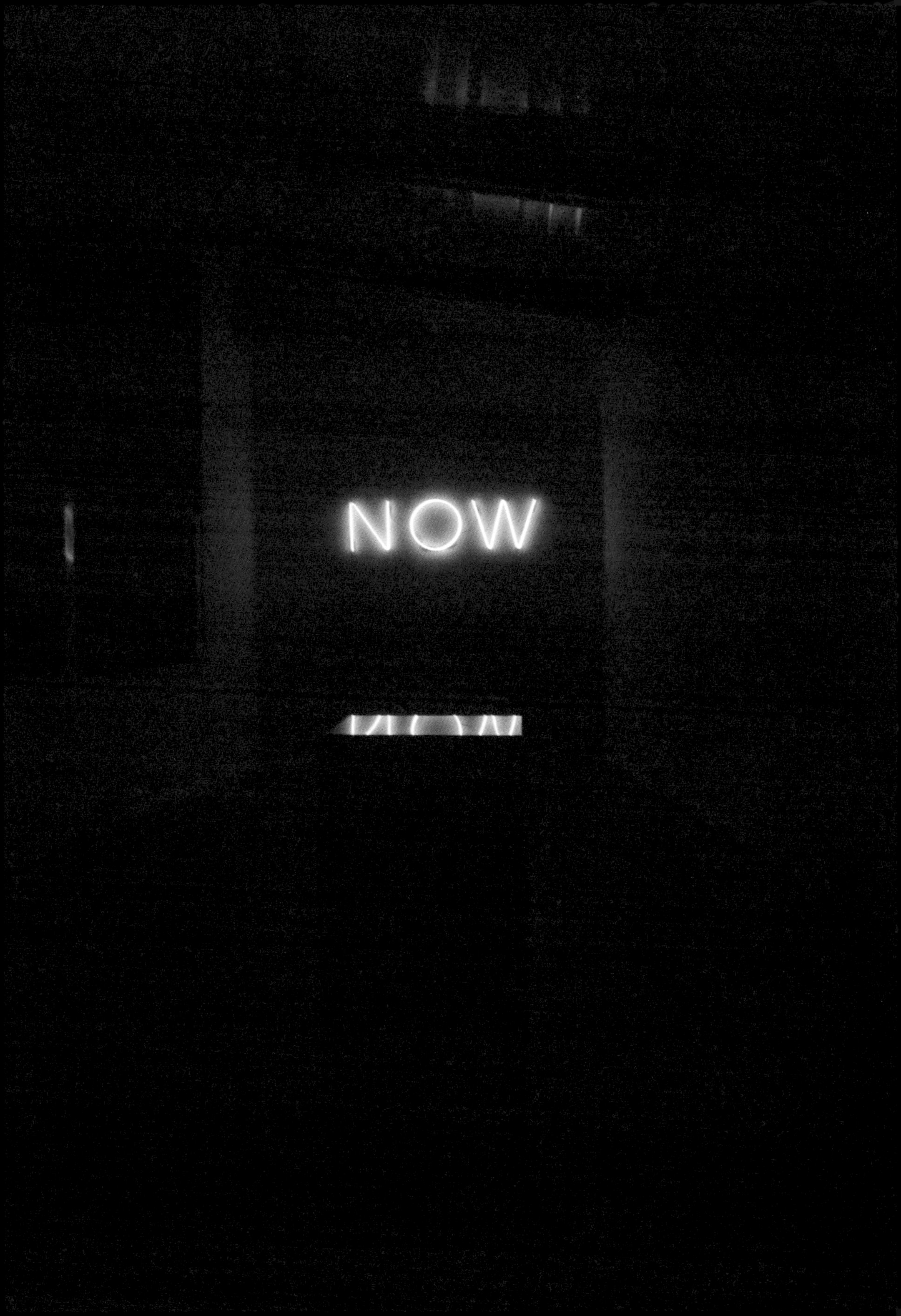

NOW

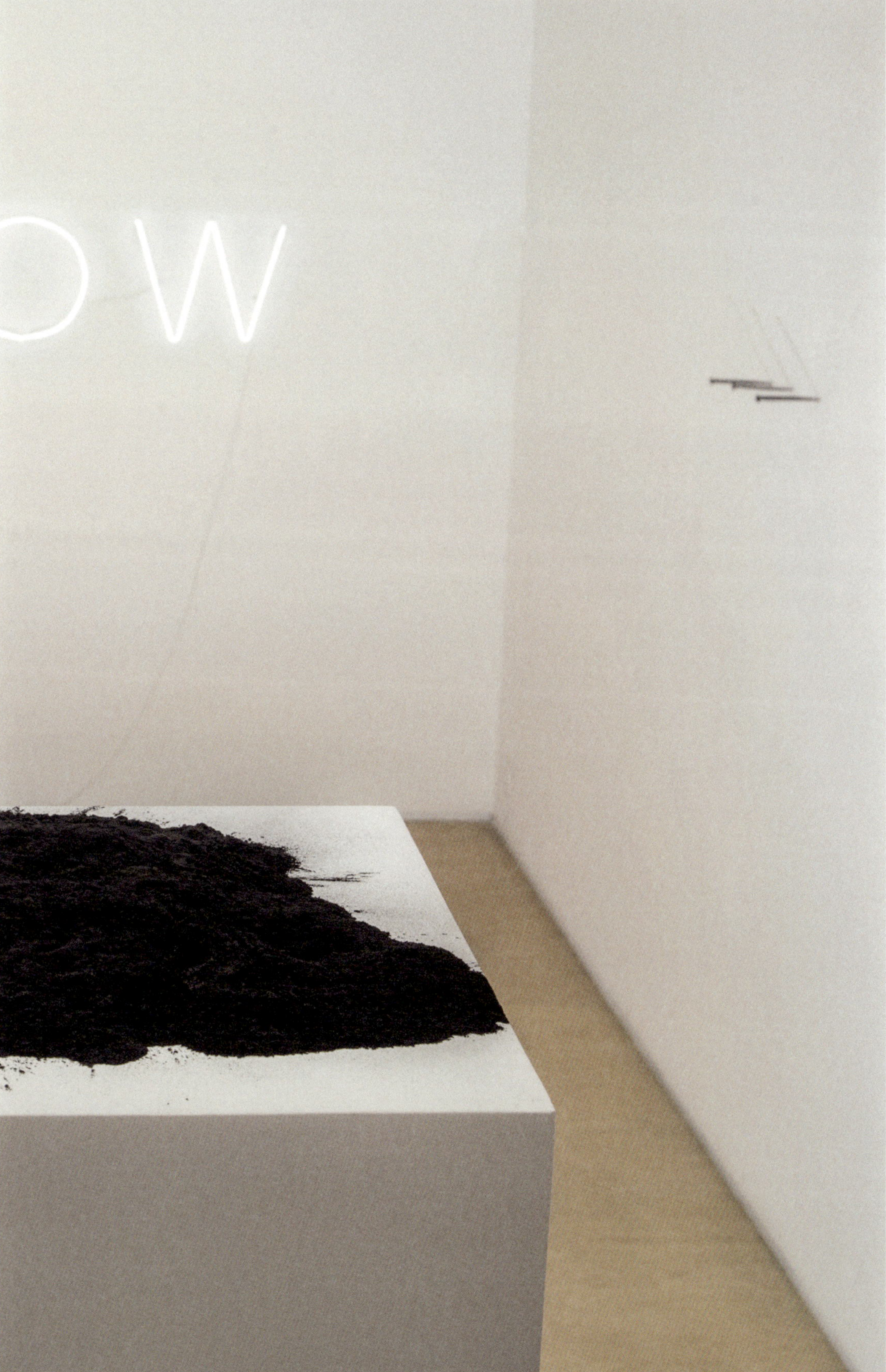
OW

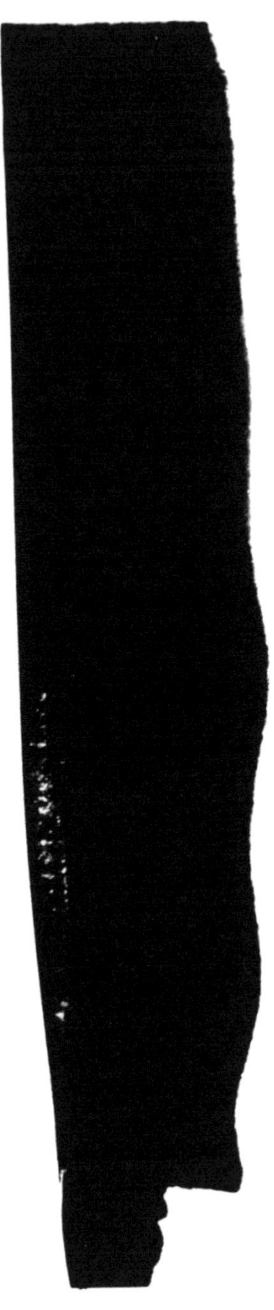

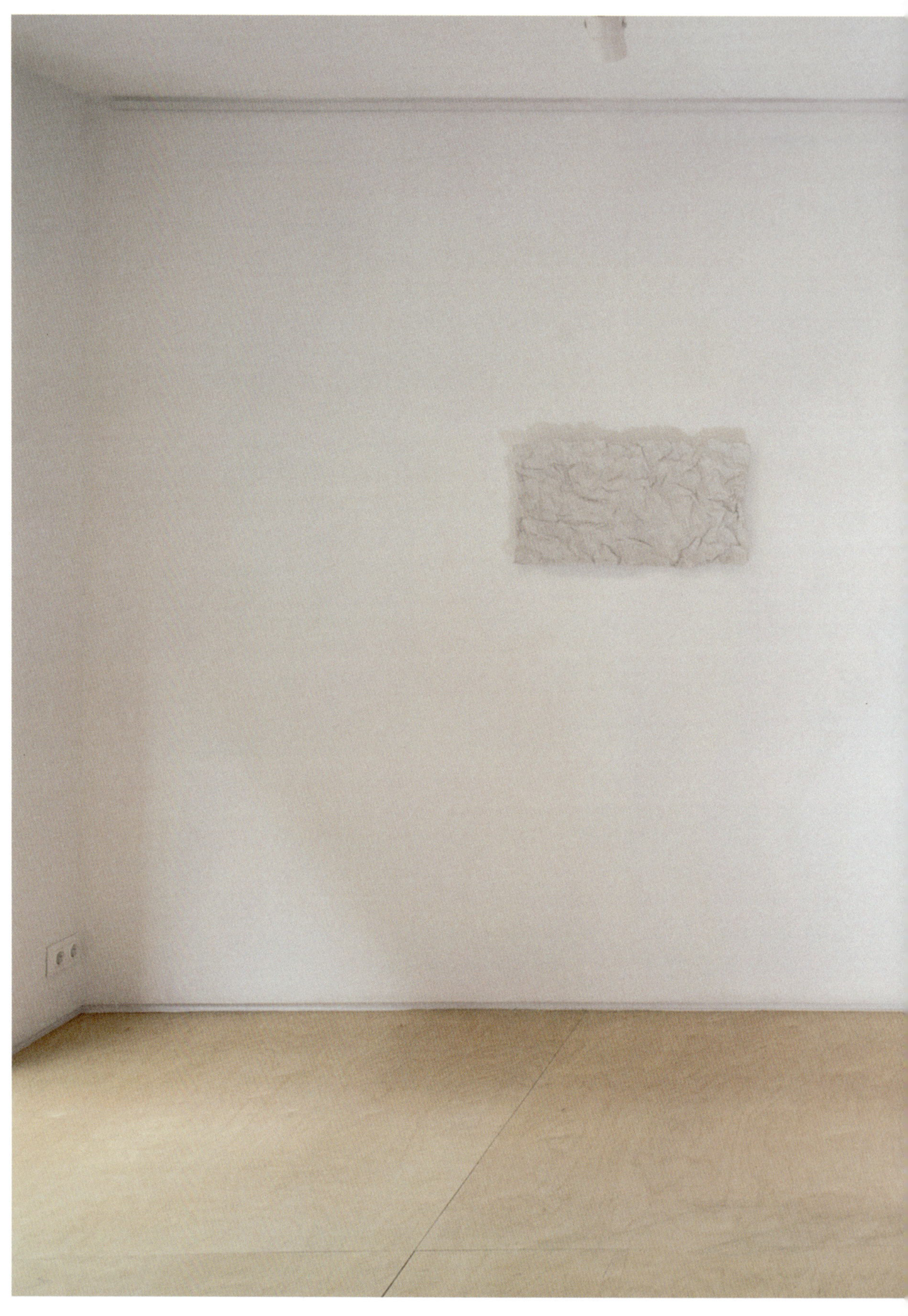

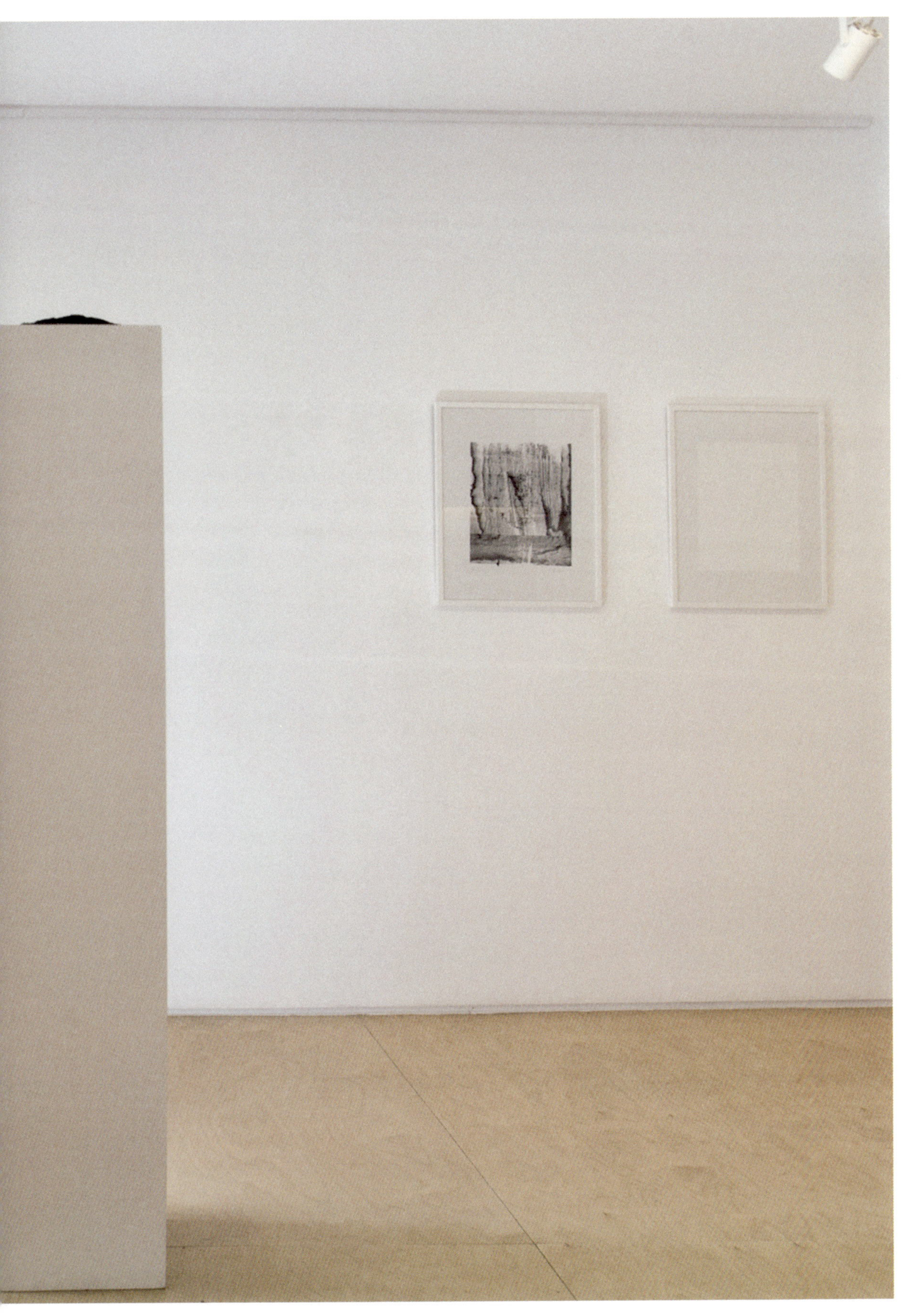